EGYPTIAN MYTHOLOGY

Ra

BY SAMANTHA S. BELL

CONTENT CONSULTANT
KASIA SZPAKOWSKA, PhD
PROFESSOR EMERITUS OF EGYPTOLOGY

Kids Core
An Imprint of Abdo Publishing
abdobooks.com

abdobooks.com

Published by Abdo Publishing, a division of ABDO, PO Box 398166, Minneapolis, Minnesota 55439. Copyright © 2023 by Abdo Consulting Group, Inc. International copyrights reserved in all countries. No part of this book may be reproduced in any form without written permission from the publisher. Kids Core™ is a trademark and logo of Abdo Publishing.

Printed in the United States of America, North Mankato, Minnesota.
052022
092022

Cover Photos: Shutterstock Images, pyramids; Olga Chernyak/Shutterstock Images, Ra
Interior Photos: Shutterstock Images, 4–5, 17 (pyramids), 17 (boat), 20–21, 28 (top); iStockphoto, 7, 9; Vladimir Zadvinskii/Shutterstock Images, 10, 28 (bottom); Stephen Chung/Shutterstock Images, 12–13; North Wind Picture Archives/Alamy, 15; Murat Irfan Yalcin/Shutterstock Images, 17 (Ra); Classic Image/Alamy, 18, 29 (top); Rodrigo Munoz Sanchez/Shutterstock Images, 23, 29 (bottom); Guenter Albers/Shutterstock Images, 25; Adam Eastland/Alamy, 26

Editor: Layna Darling
Series Designer: Ryan Gale

Library of Congress Control Number: 2021952338

Publisher's Cataloging-in-Publication Data

Names: Bell, Samantha S., author.
Title: Ra / by Samantha S. Bell
Description: Minneapolis, Minnesota : Abdo Publishing, 2023 | Series: Egyptian mythology | Includes online resources and index.
Identifiers: ISBN 9781532198717 (lib. bdg.) | ISBN 9781644947791 (pbk.) | ISBN 9781098272364 (ebook)
Subjects: LCSH: Ra (Egyptian deity)--Juvenile literature. | Egypt--Religion--Juvenile literature. | Gods, Egyptian--Juvenile literature. | Mythology, Egyptian--Juvenile literature.
Classification: DDC 932.01--dc23

CONTENTS

CHAPTER 1
The Creation of the World 4

CHAPTER 2
The Sun God 12

CHAPTER 3
The Sun God and His Sons 20

Legendary Facts 28
Glossary 30
Online Resources 31
Learn More 31
Index 32
About the Author 32

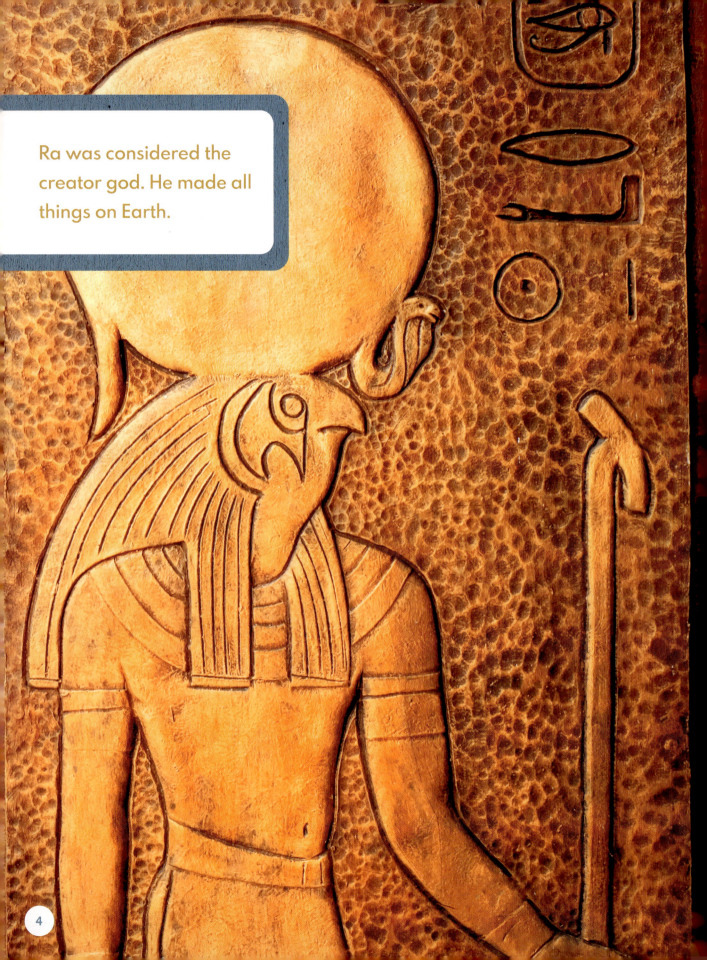

Ra was considered the creator god. He made all things on Earth.

THE CREATION OF THE WORLD

Before the world came to be, the universe was in a state of watery darkness. From this water came the creator god Ra, also known as Re. He was so powerful that he created himself.

An island also came from the water, giving Ra a place to live. Ra then created two more Egyptian gods. They were Shu, the god of air, and Tefnut, the goddess of moisture. They had two children. They were Geb, the god of Earth, and Nut, the goddess of the sky. More gods and goddesses were born. Ra became king of the gods.

Ra continued to make all things on Earth. One day, Ra's eye separated from him. Ra sent two gods to bring it back. But the eye did not want to come. When it struggled with the gods, it began to cry. Humans formed from the tears.

Ra was king of the gods. He ruled over all of them.

The people needed a leader. Ra took on a human form to rule them. He became Egypt's first pharaoh, or king.

Stories to Live By

Ancient Egypt became a civilization around 5,000 years ago. It was a complex, organized society that lasted for thousands of years. The ancient Egyptians told many stories like the one

A Protective Eye

The ancient Egyptians made special pieces of jewelry called amulets. They believed the amulets helped protect them. One amulet was called the *wedjat* eye. If the amulet was of a right eye, it represented the eye of Ra. A fierce lioness goddess kept evil away from people who wore this eye.

The ancient Egyptians left behind many clues about their vast society.

about Ra. They used these stories to explain what happened in the world. These stories are called myths. Myths were used in ancient Egyptian religion and throughout their **culture**.

Ra was a powerful god.

Ra was the most powerful god in all his myths. One of the stories about Ra explains how the world was created. Other myths tell how he made nature and society. These are called the creation myths. Ra also played an important role in many other myths.

Explore Online

Visit the website below. Does it give any new information about the ancient Egyptian creation story that wasn't in Chapter One?

What Did the Ancient Egyptians Believe in?

abdocorelibrary.com/ra

Ra took on many different forms. He often was shown with the head of a falcon.

THE SUN GOD

Ra was the king of all the gods. He was also the god of the sun. He controlled the sun's movement. As the creator, Ra could take on different forms. One of those forms was the sun itself.

When the sun came up at dawn, Ra sometimes became a falcon flying into the sky. Other times, he turned into a scarab beetle. The beetle came up from the desert sand just like the sun came up from the horizon. At noon, he became the round sun. At sunset, he became an old ram, ready to go to the **afterlife**. The sun would then disappear from the sky.

Sailing Across the Sky

Ra's rule on Earth lasted for thousands of years. The humans and the gods lived in peace. But as Ra grew older, the people decided to fight against him. Ra asked his eye for help. The eye turned into a powerful goddess named Hathor.

Ra, *left*, sailed across the sky in his sun boat. Sometimes, other gods rode with him.

She took the form of a lioness, called Sekhmet, and hurt many people.

Ra felt sorry for the people. He stopped Sekhmet, but he could no longer live with humans. Ra decided he was too old and tired to rule them. He began sailing across the sky in a great ship. For 12 hours, he traveled from the east to the west. This made up the 12 hours of daylight. Ra brought light to the world and allowed things to grow.

The Beetle in the Sky

Ancient Egyptians connected scarab beetles with Ra. Scarab beetles roll balls of **dung** and lay eggs in them. This reminded the Egyptians of the sun rolling across the sky. When the young beetles hatch, they suddenly appear in the dung. This was like Ra creating himself.

Ra Sails On

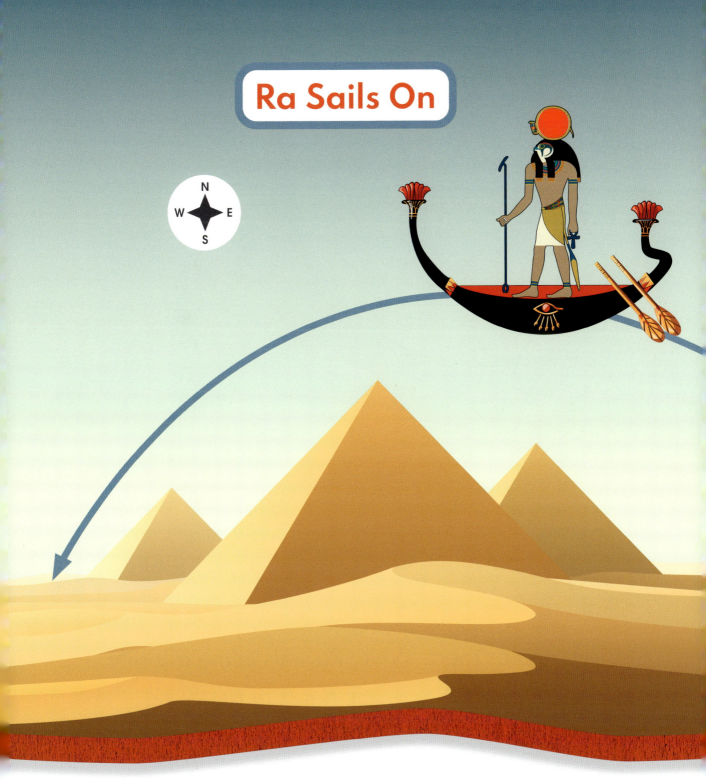

Ra sailed his sun boat across the sky from east to west. This was daytime. Then he continued on. He sailed beneath the sea and into the afterlife. During this time, it was night on Earth.

In his boat, Ra would bring light to the people in the afterlife.

Then Ra sailed to the afterlife. He brought light to the people who had died. He defeated his enemies there. While Ra was in the afterlife, it was nighttime on Earth. After 12 hours, he returned to the sky. When the sun came up again, it represented life starting over.

PRIMARY SOURCE

The ancient Egyptians sang holy songs, called hymns, to honor Ra. Part of one says:

> Who brought light to the world at the Creation,
>
> great Sundisk who brightens the sunbeams;
>
> Who offers himself so that all men may live,
>
> sailing about above without being wearied.

Source: John L. Foster. *Hymns, Prayers, and Songs: An Anthology of Ancient Egyptian Lyric Poetry.* Scholars Press, 1995. 65.

Comparing Texts

Think about the song. Do you think it supports the information in this chapter? Explain why or why not in two or three sentences.

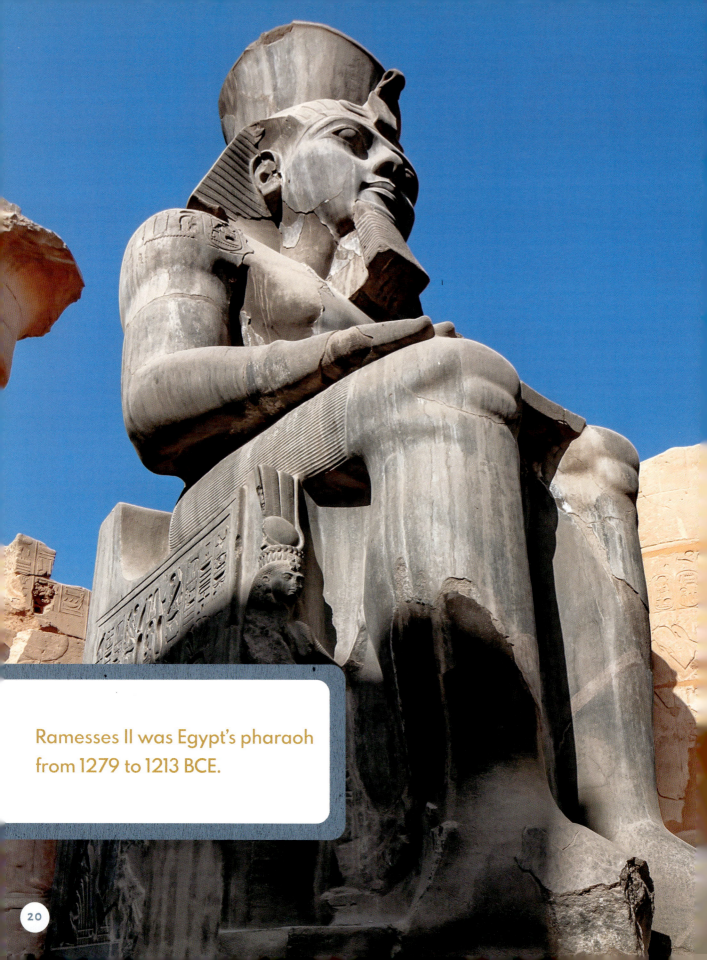

Ramesses II was Egypt's pharaoh from 1279 to 1213 BCE.

CHAPTER **3**

THE SUN GOD AND HIS SONS

The kings of Egypt were called pharaohs. They were the religious and political leaders of the country. Pharaohs participated in religious **ceremonies**. They made laws and ruled the land.

The ancient Egyptians believed each pharaoh was a son of Ra. Most pharaohs were men. Only a few women ever ruled in ancient Egypt. Like Ra, the ruling pharaoh was thought to be a god. But he had a human body. Many pharaohs included Ra in their names.

Ancient Egyptians believed that when a pharaoh died, he went to the afterlife. There, his actions were judged. If they were good, he was changed into a form of Ra. That way, the pharaoh could enjoy the afterlife. Pharaohs would become part of the crew on Ra's boat. They could sail forever with the gods on the boat.

Egyptians believed pharaohs like Ramesses II were sons of Ra.

Throughout the Ages

The ancient Egyptians built huge **tombs** called pyramids. They put some of the pharaohs in these tombs when they died. Each side of the pyramid was shaped like a triangle. They represented the rays of the sun or a stairway to the sun.

Monuments to Ra

The ancient Egyptians built tall **monuments** called obelisks. They had four sides with a small pyramid at the top that pointed to the sky. The obelisks represented Ra and the power of the pharaoh. The city of Heliopolis was once a center of worship of Ra. It had dozens of obelisks.

The pyramids represented a stairway to the sun.

The ancient Egyptians also wrote holy songs called hymns to honor Ra. The Egyptians made many paintings and sculptures representing Ra. They decorated their tombs with these images.

When artwork shows Ra in the afterlife, he often has the head of a ram.

Ra is usually shown with a golden circular disk on top of his head. This disk represents the sun. Sometimes a cobra surrounds the disk. The cobra represents protection from enemies.

Ra is also shown in other forms. Many times, he has the head of a falcon with a sun disk on the head. If Ra is shown in the afterlife, he often has the head of a ram and is riding in the sun boat. In any case, Ra always represented light and growth to the ancient Egyptians.

Further Evidence

Look at the website below. What new evidence does it give to support Chapter Three?

Amun-Ra

abdocorelibrary.com/ra

LEGENDARY FACTS

In the ancient Egyptian myths, Ra created himself, the world, and its people.

Ra ruled Earth until the people turned against him.

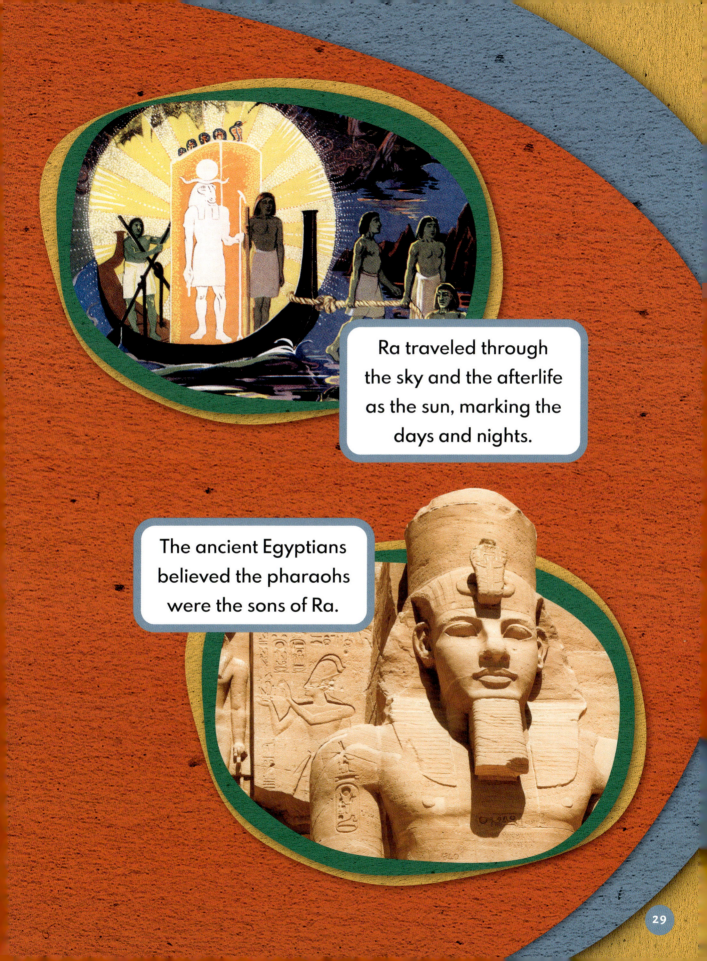

Ra traveled through the sky and the afterlife as the sun, marking the days and nights.

The ancient Egyptians believed the pharaohs were the sons of Ra.

Glossary

afterlife
in ancient Egypt, a place a person's spirit goes after death

ceremonies
formal actions and words performed during important occasions

culture
the customs, traditions, ideas, and ways of life shared by a group of people

dung
waste matter from an animal

monuments
buildings, stones, or statues that honor people or events

tombs
burial chambers for people who have died

Online Resources

To learn more about Ra, visit our free resource websites below.

Visit **abdocorelibrary.com** or scan this QR code for free Common Core resources for teachers and students, including vetted activities, multimedia, and booklinks, for deeper subject comprehension.

Visit **abdobooklinks.com** or scan this QR code for free additional online weblinks for further learning. These links are routinely monitored and updated to provide the most current information available.

Learn More

Hudak, Heather C. *Hathor.* Abdo, 2023.

Moroney, Morgan E. *Gods and Goddesses of Ancient Egypt.* Rockridge, 2020.

Index

afterlife, 14, 18, 22, 27

beetles, 14, 16

ceremonies, 21
creation myths, 5–8, 11, 19

Eye of Ra, 6, 8, 14

Geb, 6

hymns, 19, 25

Nut, 6

pharaohs, 8, 21–24

Sekhmet, 15–16
Shu, 6
sun boat, 16–17, 22, 27
sun disk, 19, 26–27

Tefnut, 6
tombs, 24–25

About the Author

Samantha S. Bell lives in the foothills of the Blue Ridge Mountains. She has written more than 100 nonfiction books for kids on topics ranging from penguins to tractors to surviving on a deserted island.